Norse mythology for beginners

Discover the exciting and mysterious myths and sagas of the Nordic world from Edda & Co.

Viktor Kulas

✈ CONTENT

What you can expect in this book

Almost everyone is familiar with names like Thor and Loki from movies, comics and other corners of the media world today, but where do they come from?

This is exactly what this book is about. You dive for a while into the origins of these well-known names - into the Nordic mythology. Thereby you can not only get an overview about the scientific sources, in order to investigate if necessary there afterwards even more exactly, than the things are spread out here, you wander besides for a short time through the mythological world, which was created in the pre-Christian time.

You'll not only get to know its inhabitants, such as the Aesir and notable creatures like the Midgard Serpent, but also some of the central elements and myths that shape this world and have been told for generations. Dare to explore the different worlds of this ancient mythology that were connected by the great World Tree, experience

You of the creation story, which one told at that time - and of the tragic end Ragnarök, which should provide at the same time for a new beginning. Take a look at old hero myths that have been handed down from that time and learn more about the great deeds that were told for entertainment.

Norse mythology may be old and vast, but disappearing into the mysteries of this world for a while while broadening your horizons is a whole lot easier with the help of this book, and soon hopefully your interest will be piqued to want to spend even more time in the legendary world after the brief overview this book provides.

A first step

If you delve into the depths of the Norse saga world, you will quickly discover that several mythologies often intermingle (and occasionally motifs from other mythologies, such as Greek or Roman, appear). First and foremost, the Norse myths comprise tales and religious ideas from the Scandinavian region, which in itself was not homogeneous at that time either, i.e. was characterized by divergent cultural views.

This means that behind the Nordic sagas there is not a single version of religious beliefs, rites and motifs, but differences are to be expected from the outset. This picture of mythology only intensifies if one then also assumes that other European influences from that time are reflected - especially Germanic ones. There are some sources from the Germanic area, which take up the mythology from Scandinavia again and if necessary modify and adapt it.

Overall, however, the Nordic saga world can be defined as originating from a time before the Christianization of Scandinavia and as being based on two different "basic principles": nature spirits and gods. While gods appeared in human form, nature spirits probably often appeared in animal form and were often associated with a certain place in nature.

The Norse saga world is a vast construct and it is easy to lose track of it. This small guide should therefore help you to get a rough overview of the research situation and the individual elements of this veritable maze.

At the center of mythology is sometimes a large ash tree that is supposed to hold the world together. Yggdrasil, as this oversized ash tree is called, connects the various realms of mythology - the world of the gods Asgard, the human world Midgard, which is adjacent to the home of the giants, Jötunheim and last but not least Niflheim, the underworld, where the realm of the dead lies. The central aspect of this own little cosmos are the gods and the giants, who are enemies from the beginning to the end of the myths and never give up their feud - with some exceptions - and regularly attack each other because of some events.

However, over all these (sometimes seemingly quite banal) deeds hangs threateningly a great prophecy that predicts the end of the world - Ragnarok. While the gods do everything to prevent this from happening, their opponents - in this case not only the giants, but also other monsters - try to conjure up the end at any cost.

Many of the myths focus on typical warrior characteristics - bravery, wisdom, strength, honor. They seem to have been the most important values at that time and clearly run through many sagas.

But now the question arises: How do we know today what it was all about and how important the mythology was for the people at that time?

The scientific sources

From an archaeological point of view, traces of Norse mythology can even be traced back to 1500 BC. In this time there are already first indications of fertility and sun cults, which have been preserved for example as rock carvings. Also in the late Bronze Age, between 1500 and 1000 BC, probably the first cremations occurred, which can be dated on the basis of urn finds. The idea behind cremations was probably to free the human soul from its fleshly shell and to prepare it for the afterlife.

Around 400 BC, however, the burial rite changes

and particularly high-ranking people are buried on a ship with their most valuable possessions. Often they were also given coins, which seems to connect to the beliefs of the Greeks, who also followed this procedure, hoping to pay the mythical ferryman Charon, who would ferry their deceased lovers to the underworld.

Finally, in the period between 0 and 100 AD, the first written sources appear: Votive stones of Germanic soldiers (i.e. offerings) have been found several times. On them short messages are found, which are however today partly difficult to understand, since they presuppose a certain knowledge over the context already. Worth mentioning at this point is also Tacitus, a Roman historian, who reports about the myths north of the Alps. In addition, there are of course other scribes who recorded their knowledge in this period, and on the basis of, for example, ecclesiastical resolutions and laws, one can get an idea of the early religious practice on the continent. Then, in the 5th century, the first depiction of the mythical Midgard Serpent appears in Lyngby on a medallion. The world serpent, coiling once around Midgard and biting its own tail, becomes a more regular motif from then until the 12th century.

In the following century, the Greek historian Prokop reports about the worship of gods and nature spirits in the north, to whom the inhabitants there constantly sacrificed. The most important god mentioned in this context was Tyr, who was known to the Greeks as Ares - today it is assumed that Tyr could have been a forerunner of Odin.

Finally, from 900 AD, the warrior class was established and the Skaldic poetry began. It is actually assumed that most of the myths that are still preserved today were only created in this period and their possible predecessor versions were only partially re-established in the recorded myths and therefore naturally went through some changes. From this time the first components of the mythology seem to have found their way to Iceland as well, because the sagas there also take up elements and legendary figures of the Norse mythology in order to interweave them with their own material. For example, there is the *Skírnismál*, which calls Odin, Thor and Frey in some curses, or the *Egils saga*, which also calls Odin, Frey and Njörd in a curse.

After Christianization began in Denmark in the 11th century and slowly spread to the north, it was then in the 13th century that the most famous works found their way into the world: the Elder Edda, the Song Edda and the Snorra Edda, also known as the Prose Edda, written by Snorri Sturlurson, who feared that the Norse myths would be lost through Christianization and therefore put them in writing.

It is based on the other two Eddas and is nowadays the source on which most assumptions about the mythology are based - however, when considering it, one must not forget that the Snorra Edda dates back to a time when Christianity was already the dominant religion in Scandinavia for two centuries. Therefore, it cannot be excluded that Snorri's retellings have taken up some Christian elements or at least have been influenced by Christianity, though not necessarily very clearly or obviously. Not to mention the narratives that were based on historical events, but obviously written down long after the events.

So most of what we know today comes from written records, from ancient historians, and from archaeological artifacts, especially votive offerings. However, many written traditions come from the higher, social classes and therefore do not help to paint a clear picture of how widespread all these things ultimately were.

But enough of the historical background - it's time to look at the content of Norse mythology - starting with some important figures.

The mythological inhabitants

In Norse mythology, there is a diverse population of people who live and spend their lives in all the worlds around the tree Yggdrasil. There are the giants, on the one hand, but also the gods and a multitude of mythological beings, some more, some less notable. In this chapter you'll get to know the most important groups and their most notable representatives in a bit more detail, so that afterwards you'll know who is roaming around in the vastness of this legendary world.

THE AESIR, CREATORS OF MANKIND

Two deities are found in Norse mythology and the younger of the two are the so-called Aesir. Twelve of them are believed to reside in Asgard according to the Younger Edda, and they are generally considered the more warlike of the two deities; they are strong, powerful - but not immortal. Their eternal youth depends only on the apples of a certain goddess - Idun, goddess of youth and immortality.

Besides, the Aesir have another special role: they are also considered as the creators of the people, or rather at least one, but maybe three of them do (it depends on whether one asks the Prose Edda or the Volüspá about it). And this one is none other than:

Odin

The All-Father and leader of the Aesir. Odin is said to have been involved not only in the creation of the first humans, Ask and Embla, but also in that of the Earth, having once killed the first living creature, the giant Ymir. The father of all gods was often depicted as a bearded man with only one eye - the other he once gave to the giant Mimir to be able to see hidden things instead, after drinking from the Well of Wisdom at

Yggdrasil -, he often wore a hat and a cloak.

He was always accompanied by his eight-legged steed Sleipnir, which could even fly, and his two ravens - Hugin and Munin. The winged duo was sent out by Odin at the beginning of the day, and when they returned later in the morning, they told the god about all the things they had seen and heard on their flight through the world, so that he always knew what was going on around the tree Yggdrasil.

As his title as father of the gods implies, he had a lot of divine descendants - among them also the thunder god Thor.

The all-father Odin is generally titled as a god of wisdom, healing, death and war, among other names such as *Hrafnáss*, the raven god. He is also known as *Wotan* or *Wodan.*

Thor

Thor was also known as Donar in Germanic culture and, unlike his father Odin, was not appointed as a god of war, but as a weather god, although he was said to have great strength. He was the protector of Asgard and probably the most revered Norse god. The god could not be found without his ever-present hammer, Mjölnir; with this he killed giants and destroyed entire mountains, while he went into battle with his chariot pulled by two huge goats. These two goats were Tanngnjostr and Tanngrisnir.

It was said of Thor that he was not allowed to use Bifröst, but had to wade through the river when he was angry, as his hair would spark and he generated an eerie body heat.

Frigg

Odin fathered his children with various women - for example, Thor with the earth goddess Jörd - but he was also married to a goddess, namely Frigg, which presumably made her the most powerful Norse goddess. Frigg, often referred to as Frigga, was the Norse equivalent of the Greek goddess Hera. She was the patron goddess of marriage, family and motherhood, as well as fertility and the heavens themselves. Among her children were not only Balder, but also Bragi, Hermod and Hödur, and even the Valkyries.

Balder

Thor's half-brother Balder was considered a merciful, peaceful and fair god, he is said to have been the epitome of all that is good and beautiful - he was the god of light and purity. Despite these things, however, he is known in mythology mainly for his prophesied death (see: How Balder was killed by mistletoe).

Heimdall

The owner of the resounding horn, the *Gjallarhorn*, was said to have a wisdom that was otherwise only found among the Wanen. Heimdall was the guardian of the gods and with his keen senses held the position at the rainbow bridge Bifröst, which connected Midgard and Asgard. His sacred animals were said to be the rams and he owned a horse named Gulltopp. If his horn sounded, then the end of the world was within reach and Ragnarök threatened.

Loki

Strictly speaking Loki was possibly not a real Ase. He was explicitly described as such in the sources, but because of his descent from a giant on his father's side it is uncertain to what he should be counted (whereby this would then also have to apply to Odin, because the Allfather also descends half from the giants).

Loki was a blood brother of the All-Father and once gave him the eight-legged horse Sleipnir; he helped Thor to get his hammer. However, his title as the god of evil and mischief was not unfounded - he helped the Aesir and Wanen a few times, but at least as often he also hindered their deeds and betrayed them. For example, he stole from Freya, he fought against Heimdall and he was involved in the death of Balder, for which he was eventually banished from Asgard. Loki was probably married several times or at least had several love affairs. Sigyn was probably his most faithful companion, who later even assisted him during his punishment by the Aesir and caught the poison that dripped down on him. One of his other loves was the giantess Angrboda, with whom he gave birth to the goddess of the dead Hel, the Fenris wolf and the Midgard serpent.

THE ELDER DEITY - THE VANS

Besides the Aesir, there was of course also the older deity, the so-called Wanen. Once they won in the Wanen war against the Aesir, but the Wanen were actually less warlike than their younger fellow gods and were considered fertility and prosperity gods. They negotiated a peace with the Aesir at that time and peace returned. Part of this negotiated peace were among others the Wanen Njörd and his two children.

Njörd

Njörd was one of the gods who was sent as a hostage from Wanaheim to Asgard during the peace negotiations of the War of the Wans. The Wane was known as the god of the sea and seafaring, he was the guardian of the sea animals. His chariot was therefore pulled by two whales - but on land they became oxen.

Njörd was married to Skadi, but their marriage probably failed because of their preferences, since he preferred the sea and she the mountains, and neither wanted to live permanently in the other's home. Nevertheless, they fathered the twins Freya and Freyr.

Freya

The daughter of Njörd was also formerly sent as a hostage to Asgard, she also came from the lineage of the Wanen. Freya was the goddess of love, fertility, beauty - she was also given many titles. She possessed a robe of falcon feathers, the *Valhamr*, a chariot pulled by cats and the collar *Brisingamen*, which had been forged by dwarves and Freya's magical powers.

is said to have strengthened. In depictions she often possessed a shield and spear and wore armor over a flowing robe. She also often rode the golden-bristled boar Hildisvini.

Freya was given the Folkwang Palace, which housed half of all warriors who had fallen in battle. The other half was taken to Valhalla, Odin's hall.

THE JÖTEN

You can guess what you are thinking now if you have already heard about the Jöten - "Aren't these the giants? Then they must have been really enormous." In fact, however, their epithet has nothing to do with their physical size.

The Jöten were not bigger than the Asen and Wanen; with the description as "giant" only a frightening picture should be created with the recipient. There is only one evidence of the excessive size of a Jöten, and that is that of Utgardloki - but this was merely a ruse.

The giants lived in Jötunheim, their separated realm ruled by Utgardloki, and their name can be roughly translated as "devourers". They are the oldest counterpart for the Wanen and Asen, they are the chaos contrary to their order. They are superhumanly strong, almost like the Aesir, and in fact even older than the Wanen.

Angrboda

Angrboda was one of the mistresses or potential wives of Loki. Her name means bringer of sorrow, and the Aesir were all the more concerned about the couple's three children, because the three monsters meant trouble for the other gods simply because of their lineage.

Ymir

Everything has a beginning, and in the case of Norse mythology, Ymir was clearly in focus as the first giant. He was created when the biomes of Muspel- and Niflheim met, together with the cow Audhumbla, whose milk he drank to live over . From his sweat and feet he gave birth to three children before he was finally killed by Odin, Vé and Vili and formed into the earth. In his blood drowned all other Jöten, except Bergelmir and his wife, who escaped and gave birth to more Jöten.

THE FATE-SPINNING NORNS

Fate and the future also played an important role in Norse mythology - no wonder, since it was only thanks to prophecies that people waited for Ragnarok to befall the world. Accordingly, there was also a small group of ladies who dealt with it - the Norns.

The Norns were three daughters who were descended from either the dwarves, the giants, or the gods; it is not entirely clear. Their names were Skuld, Urd and Verdandi. Verdandi stood for the present and the becoming, Urd for destiny and the past, and Skuld for the future and what should be - the necessary.

They probably lived at the roots of Yggdrasil at the Urd Spring, the source of destiny, and there they not only took care of the swans on the spring and the roots of the great ash tree, but also decided on the life span of every living creature.

Often *Wyrd* appears in connection with these names. However, one is uncertain from various sources whether this is another name of Urd, the three Norns in their entirety, or perhaps even their mother.

THE VALKYRIES

While Freya accommodates a part of the fallen heroes in Folkwang, as already mentioned, the Valkyries take care of the other half and bring them to the holy halls of Valhalla, over which Odin rules. The valkyries are either minor deities or female spirit beings from the Allfather's retinue and are also called shield or battle maidens.

They decided which heroes fell on the battlefield and which entered the sacred halls, and they may have been closely associated with the Norns. Their number varies in the tales from three to as many as 27; in some cases they are said to have been able to transform themselves into wolves or ravens. In one tale it is even reported that three of them flew down to earth and laid down their wings to bathe. Shortly thereafter, however, their wings were stolen by three brothers, and they kept the Valkyries as their wives for a full nine years.

MYTHOLOGICAL CREATURES

Besides all the human-like entities, Midgard and the other worlds were of course also home to more animal-like creatures - the spectrum here ranged from ravens to deer and boars to lindworms and giant wolves.

Some are companions of the notable gods or their sacred animals, as you've already learned, but it doesn't hurt to take a look at the origins of some select notable beings:

Sleipnir

Sleipnir has already been mentioned several times - it is an eight-legged steed that Loki once gave to his blood brother Odin. But who is Sleipnir and where does such an unusual mount come from? Sleipnir comes from Loki's love affair with the stallion Svadilfari. Loki had transformed himself into a mare in order to seduce the stallion, who was supposed to help build the wall around Asgard within one winter. The builder, a not further known Hrimthurse (frost giant), would have received for the achievement of this goal not only sun and moon as a gift, but also Freya as a wife, which Loki so successfully prevented.

The Hrimthurse felt betrayed and wanted to kill the gods, whereupon Thor slew him and they realized that they had been dealing with a giant.

Fenriswolf

The Fenris wolf, also known simply as Fenrir, is also one of Loki's offspring and the first offspring he had with Angrboda. He was a wolf of incredible size and Odin once took him to Asgard when he was small. He hoped that he could tame him, but the ideas of the gods were exceeded - and not in a positive sense. The beast became huge and stronger than they would have liked, so that they finally chained him with a special chain, *Laeding*. However, he freed himself and they tried *Droma* and finally *Gleipnir*, which was considered unbreakable work of the dwarves.

Fenrir had only allowed himself to be chained when one of the gods put a hand in his mouth, and when he realized he could not get free, he bit off the hand of the god - in this case Tyr - and howled, whereupon a sword was rammed down his throat. From the blood was born the river Von.

The wolf spent the rest of his life chained to a rock until the day of Ragnarok and only then freed himself to go to battle against the gods alongside his father Loki. He met his end in this battle when the god Vidar tore his head in two with his bare hands.

> *Gleipnir* was considered unbreakable, but ironically was probably made from downright absurd things like a woman's whiskers and a fish's voice.

Nidhöggr

As already mentioned, creatures like lindworms or dragons also existed in this mythology - although experts would now certainly discuss at length whether they should be lumped together in one group or not, which is probably due to the different conceptions of all mythologies. The British would certainly insist at this point that lindworms are merely a wingless wyvern, i.e. a bipedal dragon, while someone else would certainly claim that a wingless monster cannot be a dragon.

In the case of Nidhöggr, depending on the source, you are dealing with a dragon or a serpent - or even a serpentine dragon. The monster nibbled on the roots of the world tree Yggdrasil for centuries and ate from the corpses of fallen warriors during Ragnarok. He lives with other snakes at the spring Hvergelmir, which feeds all rivers and is located at the third root of the ash tree, at least according to the Prose Edda.

The World Serpent is considered by many to be the
origin of the symbol of Ouroboros - the sign of infi-
nity, a snake biting its own tail; a constant cycle
whose beginning conditions the end.

In fact, however, the oldest image dates back to the
tomb of Tutankhamun around 1330 BC - an original
form was even found during the Hongshan culture in
China (4700-2900 BC).

Jörmungand

Jörmungand is probably one of the most central beings
of the entire Norse mythology - because behind the
name is none other than the great world serpent,
which spanned the entire world. Jörmungand is
another of the three children of Loki and Angrboda and
was thrown by Odin into the primordial ocean, where,
however, it continued to grow until it could wrap
around the entire world.

Three times Thor faced it - once during a fishing
trip, where his companion Hymir cut the line out of
fear and Thor later either slew or slapped him for it,
depending on his composure - but in their last encoun-
ter during Ragnarok they both die, Jörmungand by
Mjölnir and Thor by the serpent's venom. It was said
that the Midgard Serpent bit its own tail, creating a
circle - but as soon as it let go, Ragnarok would begin.

Central elements and myths

The Norse world offers the curious reader and listener an almost overwhelming amount of individual myths, which either combine central elements of this mythology, tell of its origin, or really just tell a story. However, myths often had not only a narrative character; they were also intended to justify events, such as natural phenomena, or to legitimize kings of the time by creating a family bond between the great deities and the king - the kings were distinguished as descendants of the gods with the help of these genealogical myths.

To give you some insight into some myths, in this

chapter we look at both the creation story of the world and its fabled end Ragnarok - as well as some myths in between.

VOLÜSPÁ - PROPHECY OF THE SEER

The Volüspá described no more and no less than the story of creation and the end of the world - that is, Ragnarok. It also prophesied what was waiting after the end of the world, namely a new creation.

The seer's prophecy began with the two worlds of Muspelheim and Niflheim and the void Ginnungagap (see *Of Niflheim and Muspelheim - The Story of Creation*), told of the gods and Norns and of the War of the Wans before she spoke of *Balder*'s murder (see *How Balder Was Killed by Mistletoe*). From then on, events headed towards the Ragnarok (see *Ragnarok - The End of the World*), but even after that, the world was not lost for all time, but was to pass into a golden age for men and gods, in which Balder and Hödur ruled together.

FROM NIFLHEIM AND MUSPELHEIM - THE CREATION STORY

According to Norse mythology, the Earth had its beginning when the two existing worlds of Niflheim and Muspelheim collided with each other. Niflheim was a place of eternal cold and covered in ice, while Muspelheim was a place of heat and fire. Originally, between them was literally the void, Ginnungagap. When their icy rivers and fiery mists met, as the ice of Niflheim's rivers continued to expand, the first giant, Ymir, was born, as mentioned earlier, who fed on the milk of the cow Audhumbla and gave birth to other giants. Audhumbla, in turn, fed on the ice of Niflheim until she licked free the very first human, Buri. The latter begat a son with a giantess, and his sons in turn were Odin, Vili and Vé - who later killed Ymir. (Sometimes these first Aesir are also named as Wodan, Hönir and Loki).

His body subsequently served as the basis for the formation of the earth. From his skull they formed the sky and from his eyebrows the world of the people, Midgard. His flesh became the ground, his bones the mountains and his hair the trees. Meanwhile, his brain became the clouds and his blood became the sea around Midgard. Moreover, the dwarves also came from Ymir's body.

YGGDRASIL - WORLD TREE, CONNECTION, HOME

Yggdrasil is the giant ash tree that stands at the center of this mythological world. It is also called the World Tree or World Ash and is the embodiment of the entire cosmos. It is an evergreen, giant tree whose three main roots embrace and connect humans, frost giants and the underworld, so that heaven, earth and the underworld are always in communication. Its roots were permanently eaten by the dragon Nidhöggr and its shoots by the deer Dain, Dvalin, Duneyr and Durathor to force the world to collapse.

Under the ash tree there are no less than nine great realms, which are considered the home for different races. Not all of them are strictly separated from each other - Wanaheim and Álfheimr are equally located in Asgard, just as all three of them can be considered as separate realms. It is similar with Helheim, which is often considered only a certain part of Niflheim. It also appears occasionally in the myths themselves. One tale, for example, tells of how Odin sat in the ash tree for nine days in an attempt to gain wisdom; another tells of how Idun once fell from her branches due to a fainting spell and had to be rescued by her husband, the divine singer Bragi. Traumatized by her experiences, Idun remains pale and tearful long afterward.

Asgard, Vanaheim & Álfheimr

Asgard was the stronghold of the Aesir, the seat of the gods. It was located directly below the great ash tree, and in addition to the palaces and halls of the gods, there were also Folkwang and Valhalla, the gathering places of the honorably fallen. The Kingdom of Heaven also contained Wanaheim, the home of the peaceful Wanen.

Álfheimr was also known as Nibelheim or Albenheim and was the home of the "good" and righteous elves, the Light Alves. It is said to have been located directly between heaven and earth, that is, between Asgard and Midgard, and to have been ruled by the god Freyr. Butterflies, birds and flowers are said to have originated there, and the rings in the grass that could be spotted by dances of the Albs were said to bring either luck or death to whoever lingered there.

Midgard, Svartálfheimr & Jötunheim

Midgard was the home of the people and also known as the Middle World. It was surrounded by a great ocean; thus, Midgard could be thought of as a kind of island connected to Asgard by the rainbow bridge Bifröst and under the protection of the gods. In the vast ocean dwelt the Midgard serpent Jörmungand.

On the other side of the ocean lay Jötunheim and in it the capital Utgard. It was the land of frost giants and monsters, the enemies of the gods.

Svartálfheimr, or Black Alves' Home, was the place where the Black Alves and nature spirits lived; it also served as an underground refuge for the dwarves. In Snorri's Prose Edda, however, Dwarves and Black Alves seem to title the same beings and to be the counterpart of the Light Alves - both the Black Alves and Svartálfheimr are also found only in this version and therefore possibly a part of the mythology that Snorri himself once added.

Niflheim, Muspelheim & Helheim

Niflheim was the realm of eternal ice in the north. It was one of the two original worlds that gave rise to the rest of the nine realms, and is part of the underworld of Norse mythology. Frost, ice and fog are typical of this realm.

In Niflheim lies Helheim, or simply Hel, the palace that belongs to the namesake goddess of the dead. Darkness and cold have prevailed there and the place is guarded by the hellhound Garm. The goddess of the dead Hel herself was half a beautiful woman of flesh and blood, half merely bones, which was probably meant to be a symbol of the transience of life. Within her realm, she is said to have been even stronger than Odin.

Muspelheim was the second of the original two worlds and was located in the north. It was a realm of heat, flames and never-ending primordial fire. The fire giant Sutr ruled there, who is more often equated with Loki. The fire giants actually appear in mythology only when Ragnarok occurs and earthquakes allow them to escape from their own world.

VALHALLA

Valhalla or Valhalla was of great relevance in Norse mythology. It was a hall or palace in Asgard, which was under the supervision of Odin. It was where particularly brave warriors gathered after falling on the battlefield. There the 800 or so warriors trained every day and when they died, they were resurrected in the hall in the evening. They waited to fight alongside the gods as soon as the day of Ragnarok approached.

Valhalla was said to have had 540 large doors and walls made of glowing spears. The roof was said to have consisted of golden shields.

After Ragnarok was over, however, the hall is said to have ceased to exist.

HOW BALDER WAS KILLED BY MISTLETOE

The myth surrounding Balder's death is probably what makes the Aesir most famous. Since he was so incredibly popular because of his merciful and pure character, and his mother, Frigg, was all the more protective of him as the patron goddess of the family, it comes as little surprise that she did everything she could to protect her son.

Balder dreams one night of a great danger that should affect him and told his mother about it, whereupon Frigg moves through the world and collects an oath from every existing creature and object not to hurt or even kill her son. However, she left out a young, harmless-looking plant.

It was the mistletoe that eventually also became

the Aesir's undoing. One day Loki persuaded Balder's blind brother, Hödur, to throw something at Balder, as the other gods had already done for fun. He agreed, and Loki handed him a sprig of mistletoe, which killed Balder instantly.

Odin still whispered something about rebirth to his dead son, since according to the prophecy Balder was supposed to return to the realm of the living after Ragnarok, and his other brother Hermod traveled to Niflheim in the meantime to ask Hel to let him go prematurely. The goddess of the dead demanded that everyone mourn him, every creature in the world, and Hermod did everything he could to comply with her demand, but failed because of the giantess Thok, who refused to shed even a tear. (It is rumored that Thok was Loki.) So the Ase returned to Hel unsuccessfully, and she only allowed him to return Balder's ring *Draupnir to* his father.

IDUN'S GOLDEN APPLES

Idun - or Iduna - was known as the goddess of immortality and youth. She possessed a magical basket that was always filled with golden apples, the quantity of which was constantly renewed. These apples played an important role in Norse mythology, because they were the reason why the gods did not age and remained e- ternally young - and were basically immortal, should they not fall in battle.

The motif of the golden apples is probably based on the Greek tale about the Garden of the Hesperides, from which Hercules was supposed to pick golden apples from Hera's tree.

THOR AND HIS HAMMER

His hammer Mjölnir was always sacred to the thunder god Thor. Accordingly, it was out of the question that he had to get it back when it was once stolen by the giant Thrym. Thrym was the king of Jötunheim and demanded in exchange for the hammer that he be given the beautiful Freya as a wife. However, she refu- sed to leave her husband for the giant, and so another plan was needed. Together with Loki, Thor decided to dress up in wedding clothes - Loki dressed as a brides- maid in turn - and traveled to Jötunheim to marry the giant.

Thrym brought out Mjölnir at the wedding to bless their marriage with it - his hammer was quite capable of doing so, since Thor was just not only a weather god, but also a fertility god, and his weapon was endowed with appropriate blessings.

However, Thor did not let it get much further and grabbed the hammer, subsequently killing all the giants present.

LOKI - GIANT, FATHER, TRICKSTER

As was noted in the previous chapter, Loki was always a veritable cornucopia of tricks and jokes, most of which were anything but funny. He regularly changed sides with his actions, sometimes helping the giants, sometimes the Aesir; sometimes hindering the Aesir, sometimes the giants. He loved chaos and spread trouble wherever he went, although his intentions were not necessarily malicious.

As is known, he was also the father of the three greatest "evils" in Norse mythology, which became the main enemies of the gods along with the giants.

There are many stories in which Loki had his fingers in the pie. For one, he once tricked Idun into leaving Asgard with him, which ended with her being kidnapped by the storm giant Thiazi. Thiazi had previously held Loki captive in the air as an eagle and had only promised to let him go in exchange for the goddess of youth and her apples.

It didn't take long for the gods to notice that they were aging again and figure out who they had to thank for the evil. They immediately sent Loki to retrieve Idun, and he used Freya's falcon robe to fly to Thrymheim, where the storm giant lived. Once there, he turned Idun into a nut - or a swallow, depending on the setting - and brought her back to Asgard.

Once he probably also turned into a flea and hid in Freya's bed to steal her magic necklace Brisingamen. While he was still on the run, however, Heimdall discovered him, and they fought in different guises until Heimdall won and was able to return the necklace.

In another story, he stole the golden strands from Thor's wife Sif, and Thor then became so enraged that he nearly strangled the god of mischief when he got hold of him. He demanded that Loki return the strands and restore his wife's beauty with them. Loki then asked the dwarf Dvalin for help, and he made a replacement out of golden threads that probably ended up making Sif even more beautiful than she had been before.

Of course, then there was the ruse that led to Balder's death (see *How Balder Was Killed by Mistletoe*), which then sealed his fate and ensured his banishment from Asgard. When he next encountered the gods and again caused trouble - he killed one of the servants of the sea god Aegir at a feast the giant Aegir had given for the gods - he found his punishment. He first tried to escape and hid in the form of a salmon at the bottom of the river Fraananger, but the gods specifically fished for him with a net and Thor caught him when he jumped out of the water in desperation.

The gods bound Loki (in his normal form) with the entrails of his deceased son Narfi, who had been killed by his brother Vali in wolf form. They transformed the entrails into metal chains and hung a snake over his head, whose poison permanently dripped down onto his face.

RAGNAROK - THE END OF THE WORLD

Ragnarok has many different names: End of the world, twilight of the gods, the end of the world ... But they all denote the same thing: It is about the last battle between the giants and the gods. The gods were prophesied here to lose to their opponents, led by Loki.

Ragnarök began with the so-called Fimbulwinter, a three- or seven-year winter after which the wolves

Hati, Managarm and Skoll "finally" swallowed the sun and moon after their eternal hunt and Nidhöggr "finally" gnawed his way through the roots of the ash tree. Heimdall blew the gjallar horn and announced the end. Darkness fell upon the realms and Yggdrasil shuddered, whereupon, for example, the fire giants were able to leave their realm, allowing their leader Sutr to set the realms ablaze with his sword. \

While the Midgard Serpent now also rose from the ocean, creating floods and spreading its poison, both Loki and his offspring Fenrir freed themselves from their bonds. Loki took command of Helheim's dead forces alongside his daughter Hel. Giants from Muspel- and Jötunheim, together with Loki, Hel and Nidhöggr, invaded Asgard via Bifröst and defeated the gods.

Fenrir ate Odin before Vidar slew him, Loki and Heimdall killed each other, Thor slew Jörmungand but got too much of the serpent's venom and died himself shortly after. Finally, Sutr set everything on fire and the world sank for good.

However, as it was once prophesied, some survived the calamity. A woman and a man - Lifthrasir and Lif - as well as Vali and Vidar, two sons of Odin, and the sons of Thor Magni and Modi, who borrowed his hammer Mjölnir from the ashes. Ultimately, the time had also come for Balder to walk again among the living, and the god of light forgave his brother Höder, the god of darkness, for once killing him.

A new era began with them.

Known hero myths

In addition to all these well-known and lesser-known general myths, of course, another category should not be forgotten: heroic myths.

They were also fundamental in Norse mythology, and there are many well-known stories that were formerly spread mainly orally. Heroic myths are important to the people; they made the legendary tales all the more tangible to the listeners of the time. While the heroes of the story were distinctly often related to the deities, their stories were set in a much more tangible setting for the people - despite occasional mythological creatures such as lime worms that were up to mischief. They were meant to entertain and instill values such as bravery, and were therefore hard to imagine without.

The list of surviving Norse heroic myths is no less long than that of the other myths, so the focus here will be on only two of the longest and best known: the myth of Beowulf and the Saga of the Nibelungs.

BEOWULF

The epic of Beowulf survives today in only one manuscript and probably dates from the 8th century, while the action itself takes place in Scandinavia before the 7th century.

The story about the hero Beowulf deals with three important battles - the first against a Grendel, then against the Grendel's mother and finally against a dragon. The young hero is most likely to belong to a North Germanic people from Sweden of that time, and in the epic he travels to Denmark, accompanied by 14 companions, where King Hrothgar reigns. He had the great hall Heorot built, where many celebrations with singing were held, until one day Grendel invades the hall. Grendel is a troll-like monster with superhuman powers that also resembles the Jöten, or even is one.

The monster lived peacefully in his cave until the great mead hall was built near the moor, disturbing him with the constant noise and merriment of drinking parties and feasts. For a dozen years Grendel haunts the hall, killing people without ever being able to touch the throne of King Hrothgar, as he is protected by the gods.

Hrothgar and his people flee Heorot at some point, until Beowulf hears about it in Gautland. The latter seeks out his own king and uncle Hygelac to ask him to help before setting off. When he arrives there and presents his plan to Hrothgar, the latter is grateful, but one of his men, Unferth, is unhappy. He is angry that someone thinks he is bolder than he is, and he thinks the warrior is crazy for wanting to go into this fight without a weapon, telling him that he heard about a swimming duel between Beowulf and Breca, which Beowulf is supposed to have lost. Beowulf calmly corrects him, however, that Breca and he had swum together for five days before they were separated and attacked by a sea monster, which he had killed with the sword he had brought with him while his chain mail protected him. He had had to kill several more beasts after that, he tells us, before accusing Unferth that there are rumors that he is a fratricide.

Hrothgar is confident and they celebrate before it gets late and the plan begins. Beowulf and his men sleep in the abandoned hall and Grendel shows up as expected, even devouring one of Beowulf's men. Beowulf jumps up from his feigned sleep and grabs his hand. He wrestles and struggles so fiercely with the monster that his men fear the hall may collapse.

Anxious, they want to stab Grendel with their weapons, but his skin is impenetrable and Beowulf's decision against a weapon and a perceived advantage over an unarmed man pays off. The young hero rips off Grendel's right arm and triumphs as Grendel flees badly injured into the swamps. Grendel dies in his cave, while his arm is displayed as a trophy in front of the hall. However, when Grendel's mother, a mermaid, hears of the tragedy, she sets out to seek revenge.

Hrothgar, his retainers, and Beowulf's party celebrate and sleep in the reclaimed hall that night, but then Grendel's mother attacks. Hrothgar's best fighter is killed and the king attacks along with Beowulf and his men. They pursue the mermaid to her lair and while preparing for battle Beowulf receives the sword *Hrunting* from the warrior Unferth as an apology for having doubts about the hero. Beowulf still negotiates with Hrothgar how to deal with his own men, should he die, then he descends into the lake.

Grendel's mother immediately attacks him, but she can't hurt him because of his armor and instead drags him to the bottom of the lake. There is a cave where not only Grendel's body is waiting, but also the remains of the corpses that the two were to blame for.

It escalates into a heated battle that Grendel's mother seems to be winning, until Beowulf angrily throws away his useless sword and pulls a magical one from the mermaid's treasure, while his armor saves him again and again. The new sword immediately decapitates Grendel's mother, but the blade melts on contact with the monster's poisonous blood. Beowulf does not take more than the remaining sword scabbard and Grendel's head back up from the cave, where he is richly rewarded by Hrothgar, first and foremost with the sword *Naegling*, which comes from his own family heritage.

When Hrothgar sees the scabbard of the magic sword on the way home to Heorot, however, he sternly admonishes Beowulf to beware of pride. He advises him to always reward his followers.

Beowulf then travels back to his homeland and leaves the gifts of King Hrothgar to his uncle and king, who gives him his own property and a title of prince in return.

At least 50 years pass before Beowulf's story continues. In the meantime, he has become the king of his people when Hygelac and his son both died in battles. No one dared to attack his land during his reign, and so his people live peacefully for a long time while the king slowly grows old. Then one day, however, a slave steals from a nameless dragon to appease his master with the stolen goods. He steals a golden goblet, which does anything but amuse the dragon once he realizes he is missing something. He becomes enraged and leaves his cave, immersing everything in sight in a sea of flames.

Beowulf and his men go to stop him, but the hero wants to face the beast alone. He orders them to wait outside the cave and descends into it - but he is taken by surprise. His warriors see what is happening to him and get scared. Panicked, they flee into the woods - except for one.

It is a relative of Beowulf, Wiglaf, who, instead of fleeing, plunges into battle to help him. He wants to keep his oath and help his king. Together they can kill the dragon, but for the king any help comes too late. He was mortally wounded by a bite during the battle.

Beowulf makes a last wish for Wiglaf and has his

grave built on a cliff above the sea so that sailors can see it from afar. He leaves behind a people dominated by grief. Their future seems downright bleak, with everything pointing to the imminent end of his people, as they now fear that the other nations will attack them as soon as they hear of Beowulf's end.

THE SAGA OF THE NIBELUNGS

The Nibelungen saga is better known to many today as the Nibelungenlied in German, but in reality the Nibelungen saga exists in many different versions, some of which differ greatly from one another, appearing in various heroic sagas such as the Thidrekssaga and the Edda.

The Thidrekssaga and the version of the Nibelungenlied will be the focus of this chapter.

In the Thidrek saga, the corresponding (partial) story begins with Sigurd becoming a "hero" and one of the main characters of the tale. There are also many different versions of Sigurd's background; in this case, his mother has been accused of infidelity by her husband, King Sigmund, and Sigurd, then still a small child, is abandoned in a river and eventually cared for by a hind until a blacksmith named Mimir finds him in the forest. Mimir raises the boy, but he quickly develops superhuman strength and fights with the blacksmith's servants, smashing his anvil with a hammer. Mimir then asks for help from his brother Regin, who is powerful in magic. Here, the different versions are also noticeable, because the characters of Regin and Mimir partly overlap and the brother who finally turns into a dragon is not Regin, but Fafnir - if you know the saga about Siegfried, the dragon slayer, you are probably more familiar with the name of Fafnir.

So now Mimir asks his brother Regin to kill Sigurd because he is afraid of him, and Regin turns into a dragon and waits in the forest. However, after Sigurd arrives in the forest, since Mimir had sent him there to burn coal, he comes across the dragon and slays it with the help of a tree and his axe. The act makes him hungry, so he decides to roast the dragon's flesh, but in the process he burns a finger and puts it in his mouth out of reflex. Suddenly he can understand the birds in a tree, who know about Mimir's betrayal and are talking about it.

It doesn't take Sigurd long to realize that the dragon's blood must be to blame when he discovers that the skin on his finger has become horny. Without further ado, he coats himself from head to toe with the blood, but fails to reach a point between his shoulders that will later become his Achilles' heel.

Sigurd returns to Mimir and kills him, although he gives him quality equipment and promises him a horse from the farm of Brynhild, who is known to breed the best horses. Sigurd sets off for her castle and meets the lady of the castle, who for some reason knows everything about him - including who his parents are - and gives him her best horse. With these gifts, the boy moves on to Bertanga Land and becomes a standard bearer under King Isung.

Later, during a banquet at the court of King Thidrek, the family members of the Nibelungen (also Niflungs) decide to challenge King Isung and his sons to duels. So Sigurd now also meets the present Niflungs Gunnar, Hogni and Gernoz - he fights at the end against Thidrek, whose victory, however, he voluntarily acknowledges after he has to recognize that he was outwitted. He joins Thidrek's retinue, which signifies the next stage of his journey: now he moves to the land of the Niflungs, where he meets and marries Grimhild, who is Gunnar's and Hogni's sister. During his wedding, Sigurd tells Gunnar about the most beautiful woman in the world - Brynhild - and the two travel together with Thidrek and Hogni to her court in Seegard.

Brynhild agrees to marry Gunnar - presumably because she is angry with Sigurd after he jilted her as an engaged woman (although no engagement ever appears in any version).

Brynhild, like Sigurd, is unnaturally strong as long as she has not yet been deflowered - some versions report that she is supposed to be a Valkyrie whom Odin punished for not bringing him the right warriors to Valhalla. So, with her frightening strength, she hangs Gunnar on a nail in the wall not only on her wedding night, but several nights in a row, until her (not-yet) husband complains to Sigurd, who promises his friend to help him. Thereupon the hero uses the protection of darkness, sneaks into her chamber and deflowered her for his friend, whereupon she loses her powers.

A longer time passes, during which the realm of the Nibelungs flourishes under Sigurd. The next crisis only approaches when Brynhild demands that Grimhild be allowed to climb the high seat in the hall alone, which angers Grimhild because she considers herself equal to the other queen and the seat belongs to her mother. Brynhild becomes furious and accuses her that her husband had run after a hind, whereupon Grimhild opens up to her that she knows about the shame that not even her own husband had deflowered her, but

Sigurd:

He shows her in confirmation the ring that Sigurd once took from her. Brynhild had already suspected something similar and demands Sigurd's death - but only because he had involved Grimhild in this disgrace. She incites the Niflungs against him and his rising power, claiming that he will wrest power from them. So it happens that Hogni thrusts a spear between his shoulder blades while hunting, while Sigurd wants to drink at a brook - Sigurd dies.

After Sigurd's death, Grimhild believes she knows who killed her husband, but she does not manage to find sure proof; not even when she holds a so-called Bahr trial, as Gunnar takes an oath against Hogni being responsible. Grimhild sinks into her grief, while Brynhild becomes a kind of counterpart to her as a proud ruler. Grimhild, meanwhile, begins to plot revenge and hires foreign warriors with the help of her morning gift, which she still has from her marriage to Sigurd.

When 13 years later King Attila asks her to marry him, she initially refuses, because she is still too much in mourning and wants to continue doing so. But her brothers advise her to marry the currently most powerful man in the world - except for Hogni, who smells trouble. But too late - the two marry and Grimhild gives him a son.

After another 13 years Attila gets her to hold a feast with her brothers and Hogni, who of course suspect a trap, but go anyway, since Hogni had probably been a hostage at Attila's court in the past and didn't want to look like a coward now. On the way, they are told a prophecy that foretells their doom - Hogni does everything he can to make it ineffective, but it seems inevitable. This circumstance is not improved when King Thidrek, who has been expelled from his own kingdom, rides out to meet them and reports that Grimhild still weeps for Sigurd every day.

When they arrive at the court, Hogni taunts them and refuses to lay down his arms, so Grimhild unsuccessfully tries to incite some of Attila's warriors against the Niflungs and get them to fight. Attila, meanwhile, still suspects nothing, but the insult of refusal leaves him cold; he makes his supremacy clear by making them wait a long time in the courtyard.

The next day, Grimhild tries to goad Attila's brother with gifts to kill Hogni, but he refuses. So do her brothers when she tries to get them to turn away from Hogni. Only a short time later, however, Attila's brother challenges Hogni's brother to a duel, who wins the fight and makes his way through a crowd of angry Huns to report to his brother. Hogni becomes enraged and kills Grimhild's son, with which the war finally breaks out.

With Thidrek's help, Grimhild and Attila escape the hall, but the remaining heroes gradually fall victim to the fight. Rodingeir, the former wooer who delivered Attila's offer to Grimhild at the time, and whose daughter was betrothed to Gislher - making him now beholden to both sides - becomes the linchpin of the battle. He decides on his fealty and duty, but still gives his shield to Hogni, thus remaining loyal to both sides. Hogni's troops then abandon Rudiger's men, but Gernoz's do not, and he and Rodingeir kill each other.

Rodingeir's death hits the Huns hard. Thidrek sends his old master-at-arms to recover the body, but contrary to his request, he is accompanied by some young warriors who do not put up with the ensuing mockery that they are cowards for asking instead of fighting, and rush into battle. After this fight, only Gunnar, Hogni and the weapons master are left, who tells Thidrek about what happened. Thidrek grieves, but equally the loss makes him brave and he demands justice from the remaining Niflungs - he would even be satisfied if they surrendered.

Hogni refuses. Thereupon Thidrek fights them both and Hogni is seriously wounded. He asks Thidrek for one last night with a woman, whom he tells the next morning to name the son she has conceived Aldrian and to give him the key to Sigurd's cellar one day.

Meanwhile, Gunnar is thrown into a pit of snakes by Attila and Grimhild kills her last brother Gislher, who is also badly wounded, with a burning log which she thrusts into his throat. The Huns are shocked by her diabolical deed and Attila himself demands her death. Time passes and one day the gold-hungry Attila also meets his fate at the hands of Hognis' son.

The Nibelungenlied deals with some sections differently than the Thidrekssaga. Not to mention the changed names (Kriemhild, Siegfried, Gunther, Hagen, ...), probably the most noteworthy is that Brynhild/Brünhild is outwitted twice in that version, because Gunnar/Gunther also has to defeat her in several contests, which he only manages because Sigurd/Siegfried takes his place. Her deflowering also only takes place with the help of a cloak of invisibility. In this version, Sigurd also only gets Grimhild as a wife if he can successfully help Gunnar to woo Brynhild.

What is also important about this version is that Grimhild reluctantly helps to mark Sigurd's weak spot beforehand, and the spot is later marked with a cloth cross.

Another serious change here also concerns the last fight with Thidrek/Dietrich. The latter captures Gunnar and Hogni/Hagen and delivers them to Grimhild after they refuse to surrender to him. He leaves the decision to Grimhild and she gives Hogni the chance to tell her where her and Sigurd's treasure is, which Hogni once stole from her and sank in the river. Hogni refuses; he would not talk while one of his lords was still standing. Grimhild then has Gunnar beheaded and shows him his head - but he still refuses. Grimhild becomes furious and draws his sword, which he formerly stole from Sigurd's corpse, and cuts off his head.

Attila/Etzel is shocked by her act, since she had killed a hero as a woman, and Hildebrand, Thidrek's master-at-arms, becomes so enraged that he kills Grimhild. Hildebrand, Attila and Thidrek are thus the only ones in this version to survive the event, and the Nibelungen treasure, which once belonged to Sigurd and then served as Grimhild's dowry and finances, remains lost for all time.

A "Bahrprobe" was an old superstition in which the wounds of the deceased would begin to bleed again when his murderer approached the bier.

The end of a journey - closing words

So now the end of this literary short trip is reached and by far not all stories are told. There are still some tales of Norse heroes and some more of the gods who were once again led around by the nose by Loki or killed a few giants, even more stories around the inhabitants not or only briefly mentioned here like the hellhound Garm or the wolf Skoll and his companions who hunted the sun and moon all their lives. There is no question that it would go beyond the scope and miss the

point of a short guidebook to try to actually fit everything in - not to mention that it is difficult anyway,
since the versions of the stories often differ greatly or
at least in their details. Once Thor's fishing trip is in-
terrupted by the giant Hymir, once the thunder god
may hit the great Midgard serpent on the head with his
hammer. Once there is talk of Freya, once of Frigg.
Once Loki is an Ase, but then a giant.

This phenomenon runs through most of the narratives and in the end you can only be advised: Read as
many versions as you possibly can. The parts that ag-
ree will have belonged truthfully to the respective
myth in any case and those that deviate from each
other must be looked at just particularly critically.

That being said, even with the popular and much
quoted Snorra-Edda, one should not lose sight of when
it was written. It may have been written to capture the
Norse saga world as faithfully as possible for the rest
of time, but it will probably never be possible to clarify
whether it really did. Not only because of the temporal
distance from historically inspired tales, but also because of the Christian influences that even Snorri Sturluson was already under.

Don't lose sight of such aspects and hopefully you
will continue to learn new things about Norse

mythology and never stop learning, should your interest now be piqued.

May the old gods watch over you!

Literature

• Coleman, J. A.: The Dictionary of Mythology. An A-Z of Themes, Legends and Heroes. London 2019.

• De Vries, J.: Heldenlied und Heldensage. Bern 1961.

• Ellmers, D.: Die archäologischen Quellen zur Germanischen Religionsgeschichte. In: Beck, H.; Ellmers, D.; Schier, K. (eds.): Germanische Religionsgeschichte. Sources and source problems. Berlin 1992.

• Gaiman, N.: Nordic myths and sagas. Eichborn 2017.

• Grimm, J.: German Mythology. Wiesbaden 2007.

• Hansen, W. (ed.): Beowulf. The Heroic Epic of the North. Daun 2021.

• Heiberg, J. L.: Nordic Mythology. From the Edda and Oehlenschläger's mythical poems. Hamburg 2019.

• Heinzle, J: Das Nibelungenlied und die Klage. After the manuscript 857 of the Abbey Library of St. Gall. Berlin 2015.

• Heinzle, J.: Die Nibelungen. Song and Saga. Darmstadt 2012.

• Heinzle, J.; Klein, K.; Obhof, U. (eds.): Die Nibelungen. Saga, epic, myth. Wiesbaden 2003.

• Hube, H.-J.: Beowulf. The Anglo-Saxon heroic epic. New prose translation, original text, verse-faithful staff rhyme version. Wiesbaden 2005.

• Hultgård, A.: Ragnarök, ragnarökr. In: Reallexikon der Germanischen Altertumskunde (RGA). Berlin/New York 2003.

• Krause, A. (ed.): Die Edda des Snorri Sturluson. Ditzingen 1997.

• Kristjánsson, J.: Eddas and Sagas. The Medieval Literature of Iceland. Hamburg 1994.

• Líndal, S.: A Short History of Iceland. Berlin 2011.

• Lehnert, M. (ed.): Beowulf. An Old English heroic epic. Ditzingen 2004.

• Nikolai, H. G.: Völuspá. In Old Icelandic and German. = Revelation of the Seer. Frankfurt am Main 2008.

• Orel, Vladimir: A Handbook of Germanic Etymology. Leiden/Boston 2003.

• Ritter-Schaumburg, H.: Die Thidrekssaga oder Didrik von Bern und die Niflungen. St. Goar 1989.

• Schröder, F. R.: Germanic Creation Myths I-II. In: Germ.-Roman. Monatsschrift 19. 1931. pp. 1-26, 81-99.

• Simek, R.: Lexikon der germanischen Mythologie. Stuttgart 1995.

• Simek, R.: Religion und Mythologie der Germanen. Darmstadt 2003.

• Simrock, K. (ed.): Die Edda. Die ältere und jüngere nebst den mythischen Erzählungen der Skalda. Stuttgart 1876.

• Tuchtenhagen, R.: Kleine Geschichte Schwedens. Munich 2008.

• Von See, K.; u.A.: Commentary on the Songs of the Edda. Songs of the Gods. Heidelberg 1997-2004